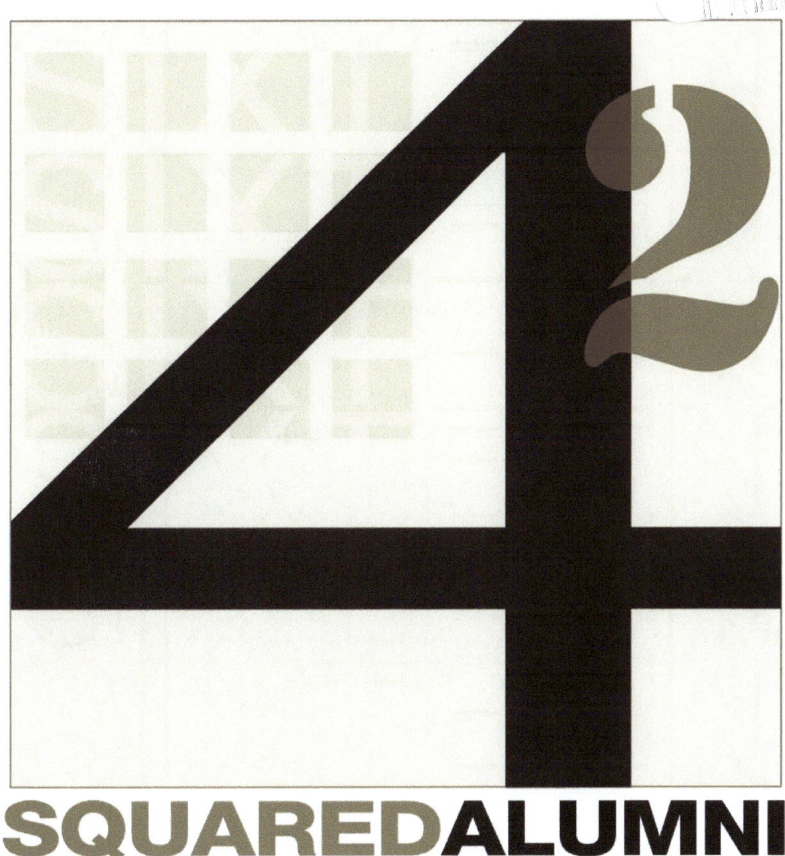

SQUAREDALUMNI

August 30 - October 6, 2018

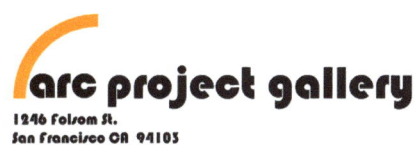

arc project gallery
1246 Folsom St.
San Francisco CA 94103

Curator's Statement

SquaredAlumni 2018 brings together eight of the most popular alumni from previous *FourSquared* exhibitions at Arc. Each artist will be exhibiting four works. The exhibition is a reflection of the Arc partners' strong and abiding interest in supporting San Francisco Bay Area art, artists and community. During fundraisers and special events, all of the artists in the exhibition will be donating about 20% of their proceeds to any beneficiary organizations. Arc will be donating 100% of the gallery proceeds from this exhibition to those organizations.

Curator:

Michael Yochum is the co-founder of Arc Gallery & Studios, along with partners, Priscilla Otani and Stephen Wagner. He is the managing partner for Arc Fine Arts Consulting, connecting local businesses and collectors with SF Bay Area artists.

Catalog designed by Michael Yochum
Logo image by Mitchell Confer
Arc Gallery © 2018

Featured Artists

Carlo Abruzzese

Robin Denevan

Tracy Taylor Grubbs

Carol Jessen

Margaret Keelan

Michael McConnell

Sawyer Rose

Charles Stinson

ARTISTS RECEPTION
Saturday, September 8th, 7-9pm

TEEN VAN FUNDRAISER
Sunday, September 16th, 3-5pm

YOUTH IS A STATE OF MIND - Bay Area Professionals Mixer
Tuesday, September 18th, 6-8pm

AMARANTH QUARTET
Sunday, September 30th, 11:30am-2pm

ARTIST DISCUSSION & CLOSING RECEPTION
Saturday, October 6th, 12-3pm

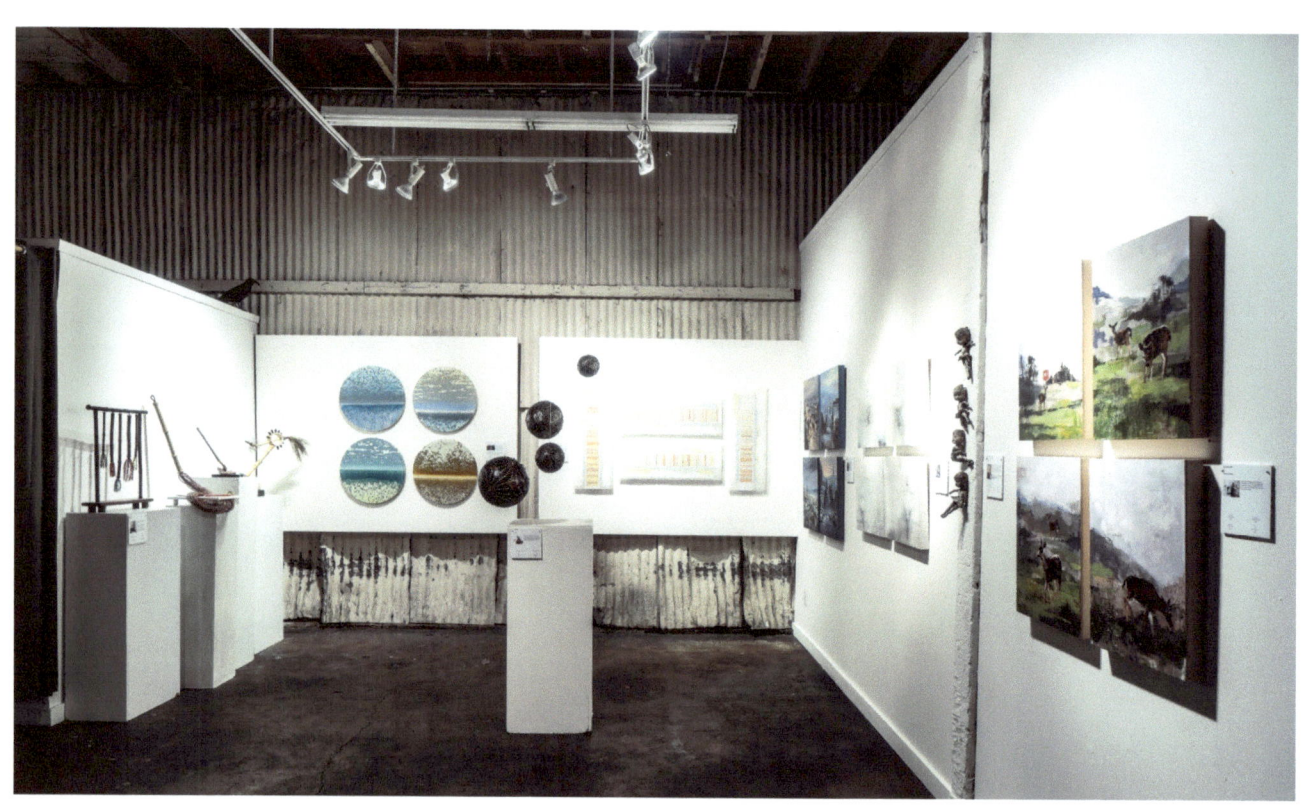

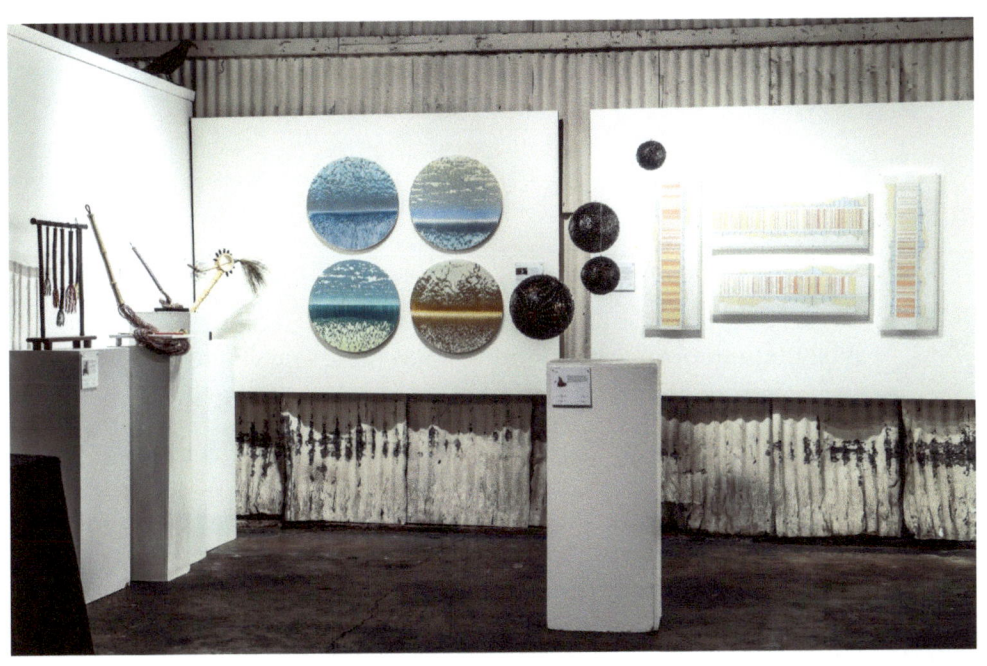
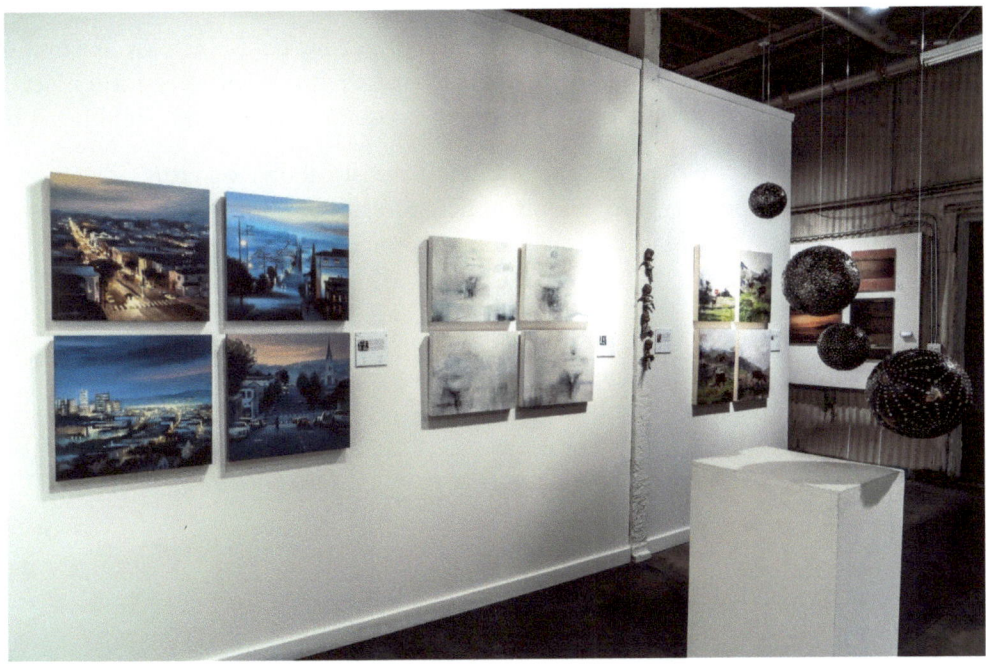

Carlo Abruzzese

Corridors

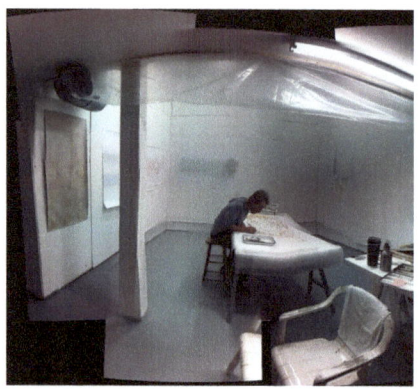

My art integrates the disparate worlds of fine art, culture and quantitative information, creating images that encourage the viewer to re-interpret the world around us.

I use simple materials (colored and graphite pencils, rulers and drafting film) to create complex, information-rich art. My process is labor intensive. Instead of using a computer to generate layouts and designs, I sort through the numbers and graphs, collate information, sketch out designs, and then draft and color by hand. This allows me to digest the information; the final product not only accurately describes the quantities, but the qualities of the new 'map' I have created.

My background as an architect has greatly influenced how I approach art. An architect takes information and translates it into built form. The intent is to make a functional, beautiful object. My art uses this same process, creating images from information that evoke discourse and insight into our world.

The artwork for this show is a transformation of statistical data on ethnic diversity, population size, density, crime rate, poverty, and income of neighborhoods along four major street 'corridors' in San Francisco (Geary Street, Market Street, Mission Street and Van Ness Avenue).

website: http://www.abruzzese.net
email: carlo@abruzzese.net

EDUCATION

Harvard University Master of Architecture
University of California at Berkeley Bachelor of Arts in Architecture
FSU, Art/Architecture History Program, Florence, Italy

SELECTED EXHIBITIONS

2017	Samsung CEO Summit, Palace of Fine Arts, San Francisco, CA
	Artspan: Selections 2017, Heron Art Gallery, San Francisco, CA
	Detritus, San Jose Institute of Contemporary Art, San Jose, CA
2016	*Access Denied,* Santa Fe Art Institute, Santa Fe, New Mexico
	Between Worlds, Arc Gallery, San Francisco, CA
	Creative Labor, SOMARTS Gallery, San Francisco, CA
2015	*Beautiful Data,* de Young Museum, San Francisco, CA
	Obsidere, Alterspace Gallery, San Francisco, CA
	Endangered Languages, Root Division, San Francisco, CA
	FourSquared, Arc Gallery, San Francisco, CA
2014	*Weaving Cultures,* Gaylon & Cullis Gallery, Greensboro College, Greensboro, North Carolina
	Catalyst, Gallery Route One Annual Juried Show, Point Reyes Station, CA
	Maker Faire, MONCA (Museum of Northern California Art), Chico, CA
	Left Brain Meets Right Brain, DG717 Gallery, San Francisco, CA
2013	*Mapping Cultural Landscapes: Re-interpreting Bay Area Demographics,* de Young Museum, San Francisco, CA
	Almost Together, David Brower Center, Berkeley, CA
2012	*Introductions 2012,* Root Division, San Francisco, CA
	DE@40, Developing Environments, San Francisco, CA
2011	*traces. threads. surfaces,* a.Muse Gallery, San Francisco, CA
	West Coast Biennal, Museum at Turtle Bay, Redding, CA
2010	*The H Show,* Root Division, San Francisco, CA
	Road Trip, 1870 Gallery, Belmont, CA
2009	*Summer Exhibition,* Wit Gallery, Lenox, MA
	Beyond Sea and Sky, a.Muse Gallery, San Francisco, CA
2008	*The Last Show,* Belcher Street Gallery, San Francisco, CA
	Reflections of the Bay, California Modern Art Gallery, San Francisco, CA
2006	*Landscape/Waterscape,* Global Art Venue Gallery, Seattle, WA
	Terrain, Studio Gallery, San Francisco, CA

GRANTS & RESIDENCIES

2016	Santa Fe Art Institute Artist-in-Residence
2015	de Young Museum Artist-in-Residence
2013	Vermont Studio Center Residency and grant
2012	Center for Cultural Innovation Creative Capacity Fund Grant

TEACHING/PROFESSIONAL EXPERIENCE

Architect self-employed, 1991–present
Visiting Intructor Department of Architecture, University of California at Berkeley 1986-8
Critic/Guest Juror Architecture Design Studios, (UC Berkeley, CCA, Boston Art Center, Roger Williams College)

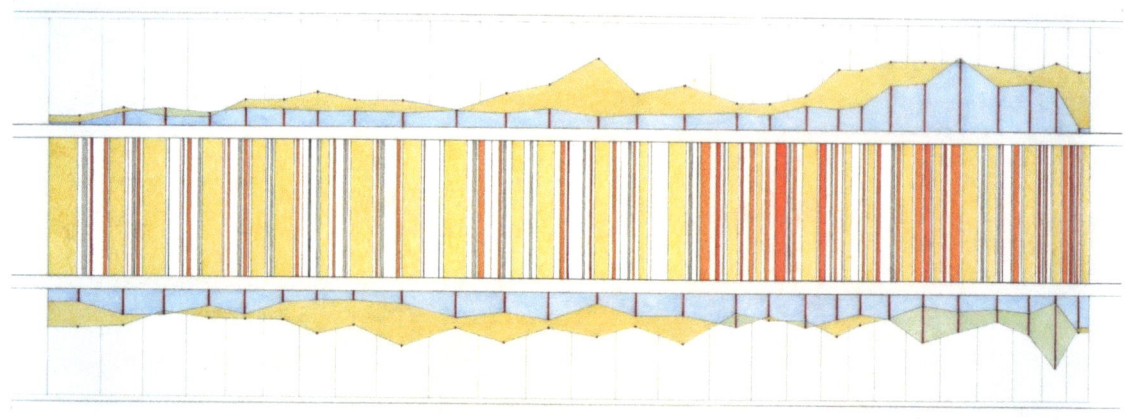

Geary Street
colored pencil, graphite and acrylic on mylar
12" x 32"
$1000

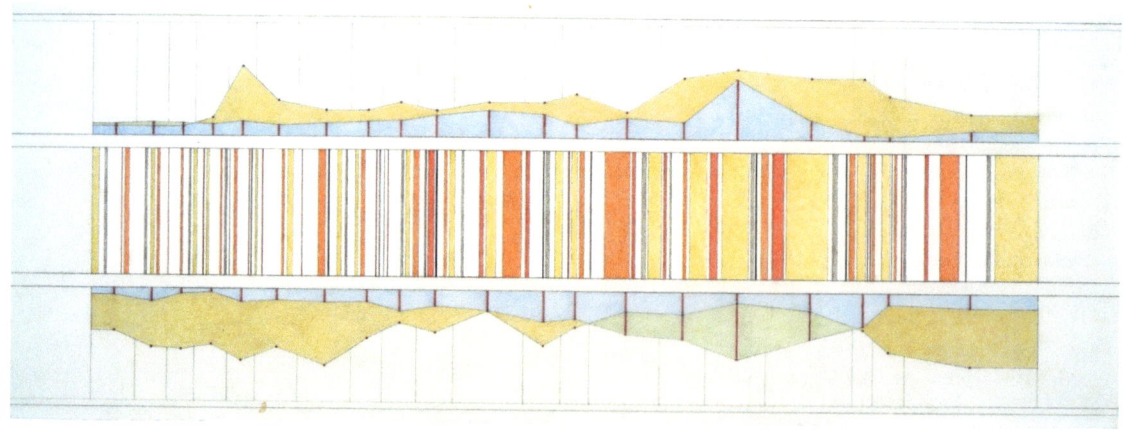

Market Street
colored pencil, graphite and acrylic on mylar
12" x 32"
$1000

Carlo Abruzzese

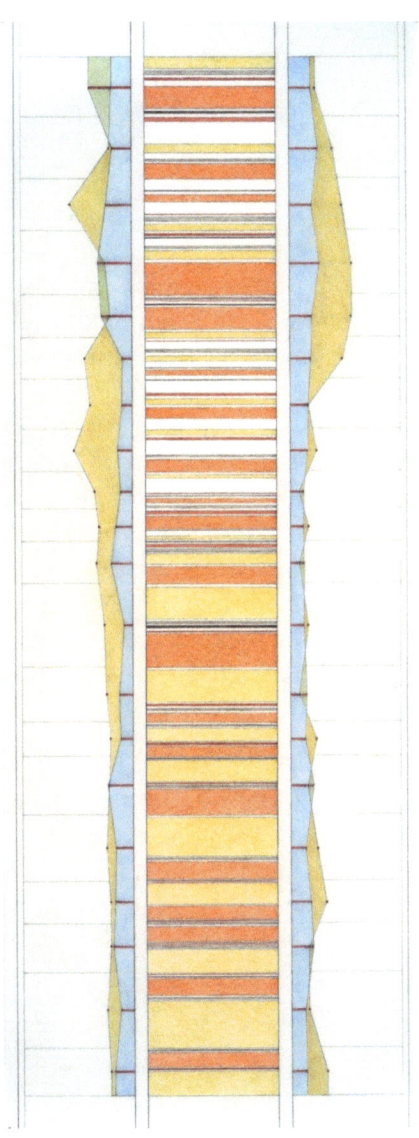

Mission Street
colored pencil, graphite and acrylic on mylar
12" x 32"
$1000

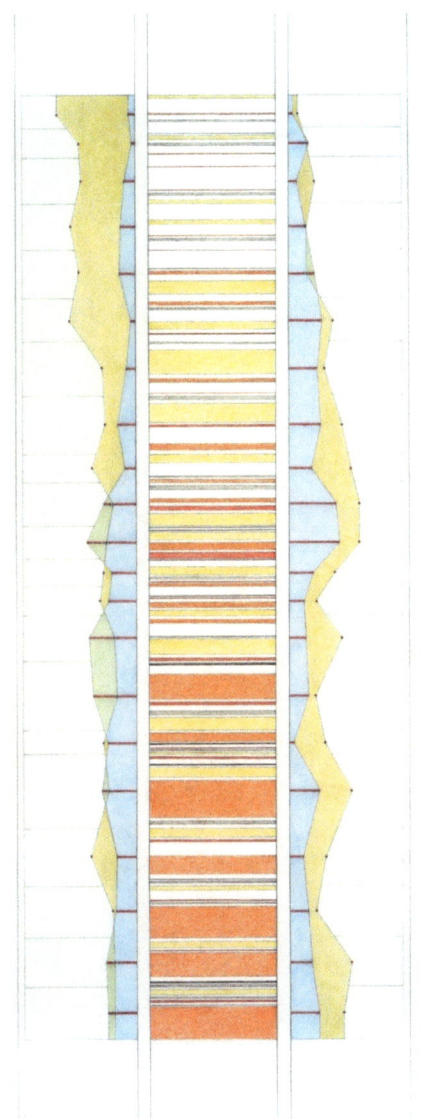

Van Ness Avenue
colored pencil, graphite and acrylic on mylar
12" x 32"
$1000

Carlo Abruzzese

Robin Denevan

Portholes to the Sea

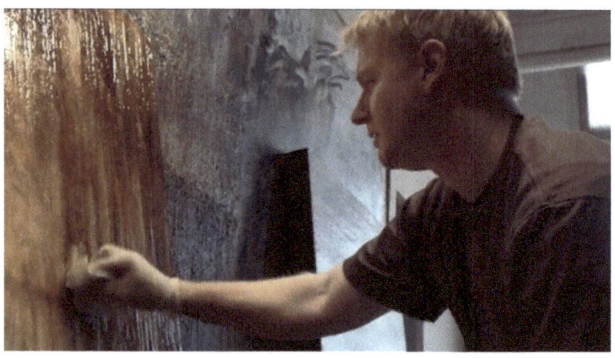

My work is about process with an emphasis on the organic properties of the materials I use and how they mimic nature and landscape. I do not render a landscape as much as I allow the materials to naturally create one. The steel series developed from this approach. I noticed the buildup of residue on the inside of the buckets I use to wash my brushes. The patinas of paint created a beautiful gradation of color and texture. Concurrent with these observations were my walks along the inlets of San Francisco Bay. My painting studio rests on the shores of India Basin. The low tides create patterns of kelp, and earth that blend into the tranquil waters.

I use steel sheets so that I can work on a smooth and consistent surface. The sheets are sanded, sometimes primed and submerged in several gallons of mineral spirits. I pour oil paint into the solution and mix it until it is cloudy. Over a period of several days the particles of oil color precipitate and leave sediment on the steel. After the oil has completely separated from the mineral spirits, I repeat the process with another color. I will sometimes sand or manipulate the surface after the bath. The painting is sealed with a protective finish and mounted on a wood substrate.

website: http://robindenevan.com/
email: rdenevan@gmail.com

EDUCATION

1997   California College of Arts and Crafts; B.F.A. with Distinction, Painting; Oakland, CA

SELECTED SOLO EXHIBITIONS

2018	*Deconstructed Horizons*, Addington Gallery, Chicago, IL
2017	*The River Narrative*, 475 Sansome, San Francisco, CA
	Works on Steel, Desta Gallery, San Anselmo, CA
2016	*New Encaustic Paintings*, Addington Gallery, Chicago, IL
	Shifting Tides, Desta Gallery, San Anselmo, CA
2015	*Solo Exhibition*, Addington Gallery, Chicago, IL
2013	*Riverscapes*, Addington Gallery, Chicago, IL
2012	*Horizons*, Patricia Rovzar Gallery, Seattle, WA
	New Encaustics, Addington Gallery, Chicago, IL
2011	*Aluminum and Encaustic*, Addington Gallery, Chicago, IL
2010	*River Perspectives*, Addington Gallery, Chicago, IL
2009	*Solo Exhibition*, Julie Nester Gallery, Park City, UT
2008	*Notes from the Yangtze*, Addington Gallery, Chicago, IL
	Encaustic Landscapes, Bimma Gallery, San Francisco, CA
2007	*Yangtze Paintings*, Cinda, San Francisco, CA
	Robin Denevan: Solo Exhibition, Julie Nester Gallery, Park City, UT
	Robin Denevan: Solo Exhibition, Bryant Street Gallery, Palo Alto, CA
2006	*Beyond the Surface*, Gwenda Jay Gallery, Chicago, IL
	Robin Denevan: Encaustic Paintings, 255 California St, San Francisco, CA
2005	*Robin Denevan: Encaustic Paintings,* Rubicon, San Francisco, CA
	Robin Denevan: Solo Exhibition, 50 Fremont St. San Francisco, CA
	Robin Denevan: New Work, Gwenda Jay Gallery, Chicago, IL
	Robin Denevan: Encaustic Horizons, Bryant Street Gallery, Palo Alto, CA
1999	*El Valle y la Luna*, Galeria Vinales, Vinales, Cuba
1998	*Nocturnal*, Gallery Flux, San Francisco, CA

SELECTED GROUP EXHIBITIONS

2017	*48 Pillars*, Arc Gallery, San Francisco, CA
2016	*Selections*, ArtSpan, San Francisco CA (juried exhibition)
	Spirit of the Land, Addington Gallery, Chicago, IL 2016
2014	*Modern Landscape*, Slate, Oakland, CA
	Material Witness, Addington Gallery, Chicago, CA
	FourSquared, Arc Gallery, San Francisco, CA
2013	*Overtures*, Nido Gallery, San Francisco, CA
	FourSquared, Arc Gallery, San Francisco, CA
2010	*Working with Wax*, Santa Rosa College, Santa Rosa, CA

REPRESENTATION:

    Addington Gallery. Chicago, IL
    Slate Fine Art, Oakland, CA
    Desta Gallery, San Anselmo, CA

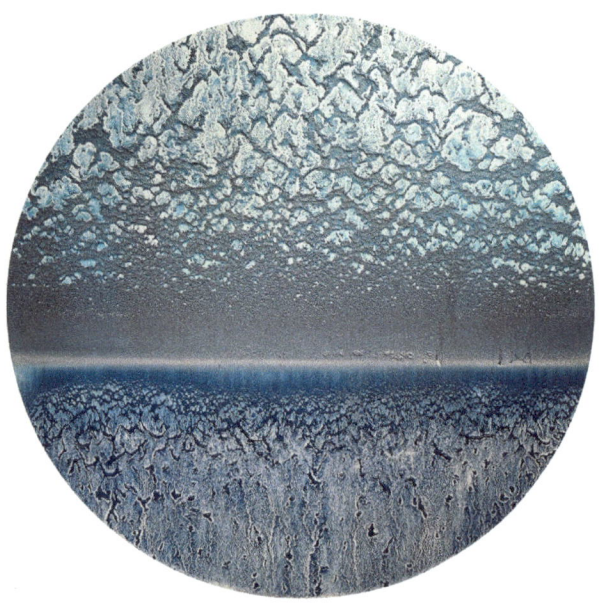

Karl
decanted oil on steel mounted on magnetic hardwood frames
20" diameter
$1500

Emerald Tide
decanted oil on steel mounted on magnetic hardwood frames
20" diameter
$1500

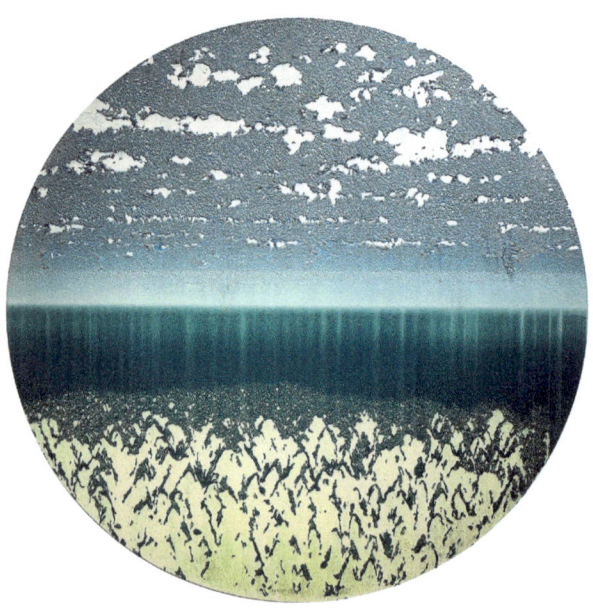

Robin Denevan

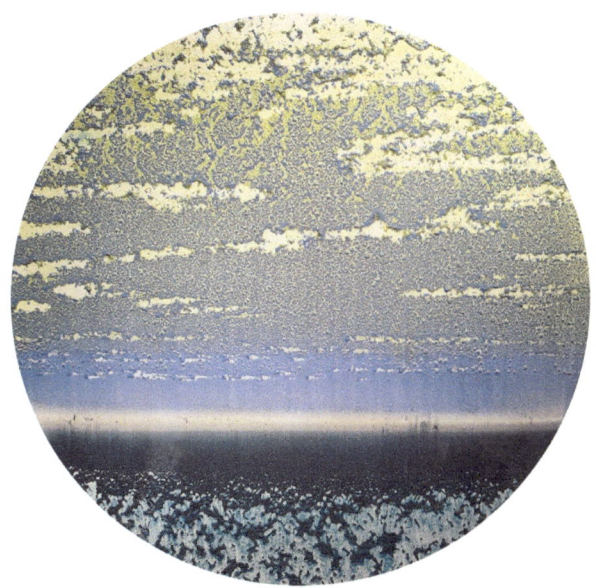

Pastel Sky
decanted oil on steel mounted on magnetic hardwood frames
20" diameter
$1500

The Sheltering Sky
decanted oil on steel mounted on magnetic hardwood frames
20" diameter
$1500

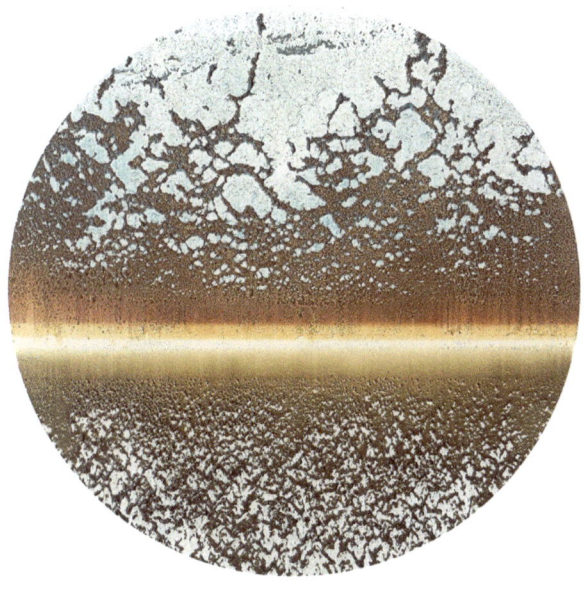

Robin Denevan

Tracy Taylor Grubbs

Ablution Series II

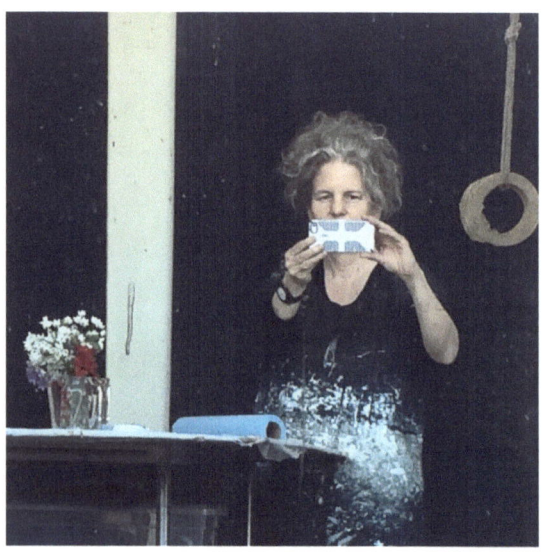

In art and in life, I seem to be searching for ways to let the static experience of a single view give way to the ecstatic possibilities of the ephemeral. Most of my works are visual metaphors that expand or deepen my understanding of the world. I draw inspiration from the power of art's silence and stillness to convey knowledge.

A sink is an object at once empty and full of possibilities, a reminder of the sacred in the guise of the everyday. It can be a baptismal font, a place to stack the dishes, a place to wash our hands. Over time, these forms have taken on new meaning for me as portals to the flow of life and the fragility of the human body.

As a material, oil paint lends itself well to the task of moving through an open field of possibility before closing down too quickly around a particular form. My aim is to use paint's slippage and indeterminate nature to glimpse a space where forms emerge within an ever-present potential for change and re-configuration.

website: http://www.tracygrubbs.com/
email: tracy@tracygrubbs.com

EDUCATION

Ongoing   International Contemporary Artist Workshops with Rosenclaire, Florence, Italy
2001-04   SF Art Institute, Academy of Art University, San Francisco, CA
1986   St. Lawrence University, B.A. with Honors in Environmental Studies and Political Philosophy

SELECTED GROUP EXHIBITIONS

2018   *Art & Spiritual Practice,* Headlands Center for the Arts, Marin, CA
           Hall Spassov Booth, ArtMarket San Francisco, San Francisco, CA
2017   *FourSquared,* Arc Gallery, San Francisco, CA
2016   Yerba Buena Center for the Arts, San Francisco, CA
           Root Division Gallery, San Francisco, CA
2015   Marin Museum of Contemporary Art, Novato, CA
           Bay Area Annual , Pro Arts Gallery, Oakland, CA
           Oppland, Kunstsenter,, Lillehammer, Norway
           Bedford Gallery, Walnut Creek, CA
2014   Hooloon Gallery, Philadelphia, PA
           Cannery Gallery, San Francisco, CA
2013   *Left Coast Annual,* Sanchez Art Center, Pacifica, CA
           Landscapes, Hall Spassov Gallery, Seattle, WA
           Small Works, Artzone 461, San Francisco, CA
2012   Shoshana Wayne Gallery, Santa Monica, CA
           50 Works in 50 Days, Sanchez Art Center, Pacifica, CA
2011   *Neither Here Nor There,* Arc Gallery, San Francisco, CA

SELECTED SOLO & TWO PERSON EXHIBITIONS

2017   Hall Spassov Gallery, Bellevue, WA
           Counterpulse Gallery, San Francisco, CA
2016   Hall Spassov Gallery, Bellevue, WA
2015   Gallerie Citi, Burlingame, CA
2014   Hall Spassov Gallery, Seattle, WA
2013   Toby's Gallery, Pt. Reyes Station, CA
2012   Hall Spassov Gallery, Seattle, WA
           Artist Collaboration & Performance, Shotwell Studios, San Francisco, CA
2011   Morris Graves Museum of Art, Eureka, CA
2010   Hall Spassov Gallery, Seattle, WA
2009   Arc Gallery, Chicago, IL
           Caldwell Snyder Gallery, San Francisco, CA

AWARDS

2017   Center for Cultural Innovation, Creative Capacity Fund, San Francisco, CA
2015   Yosemite Renaissance Foundation Artist Residency, Wawona, CA
2013   Pilchuck School of Glass, John H. Hauberg Fellowship and Artist Residency, Seattle, WA
2012   Shotwell Dance Studio Residency in collaboration with Hope Mohr, San Francisco, CA
2011   Venice Printmaking Studio Artist Residency, Venice Italy
2007   Morris Graves Foundation Artist Residency, Loleta, CA

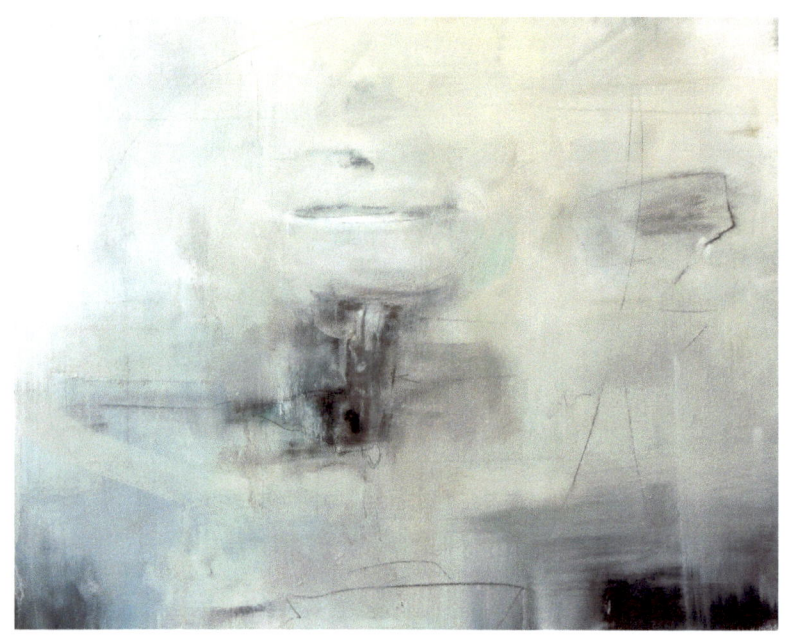

Ablution Series 21
oil and graphite on panel
16" x 20"
$1200

Ablution Series 22
oil and graphite on panel
16" x 20"
$1200

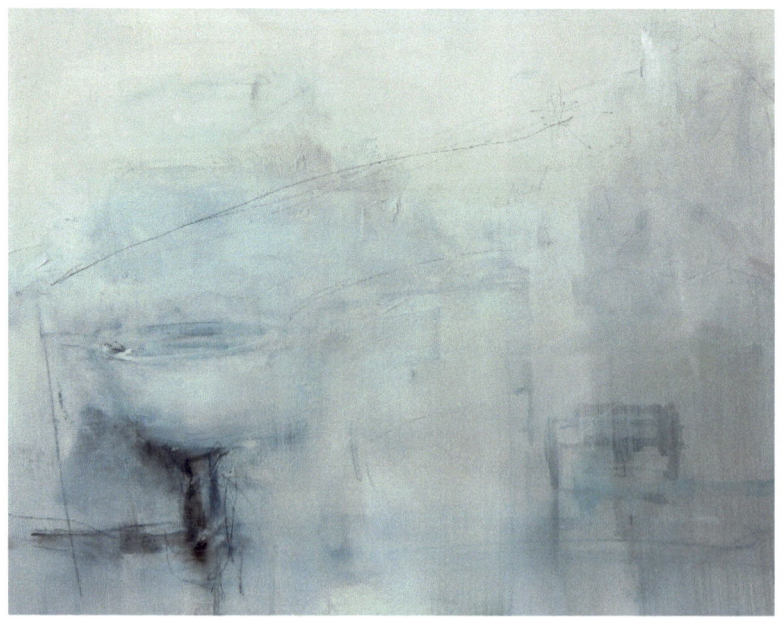

Tracy Taylor Grubbs

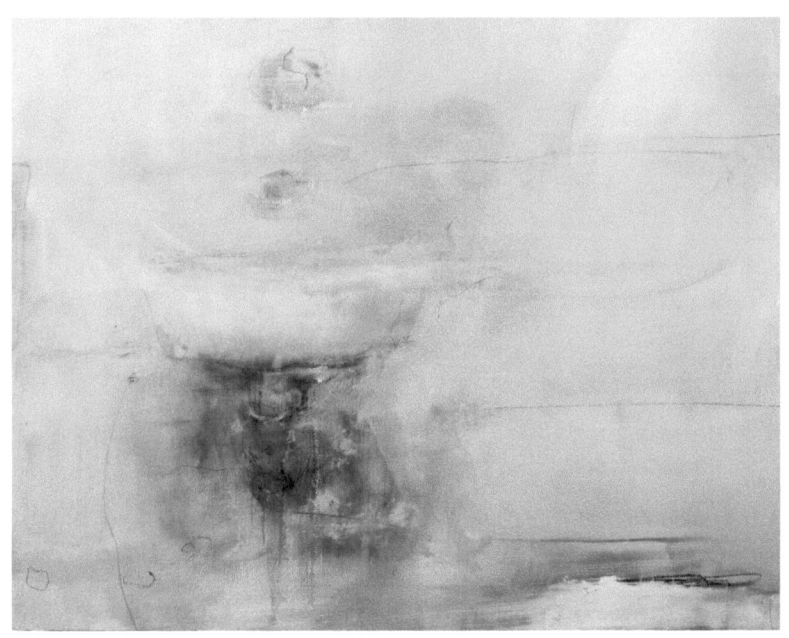

Ablution Series 23
oil and graphite on panel
16" x 20"
$1200

Ablution Series 24
oil and graphite on panel
16" x 20"
$1200

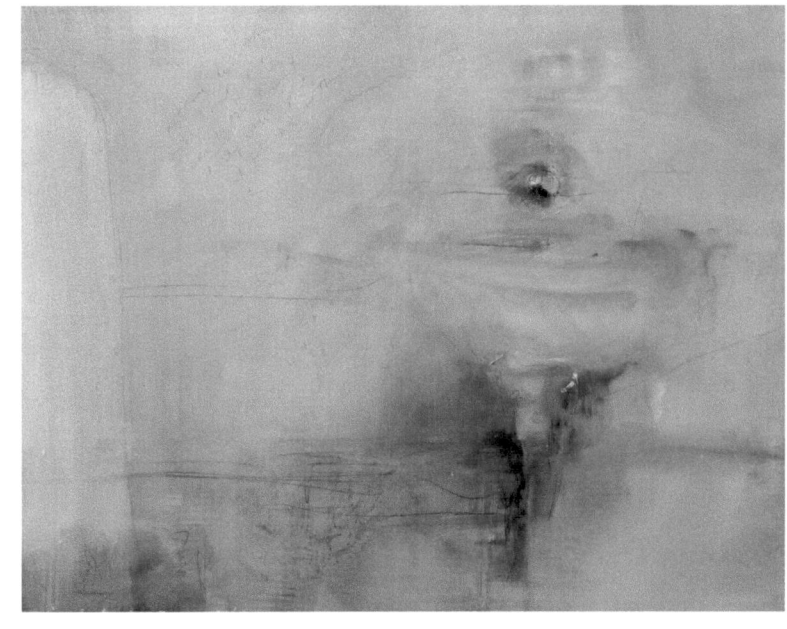

Tracy Taylor Grubbs

Carol Jessen

Blue Dusk

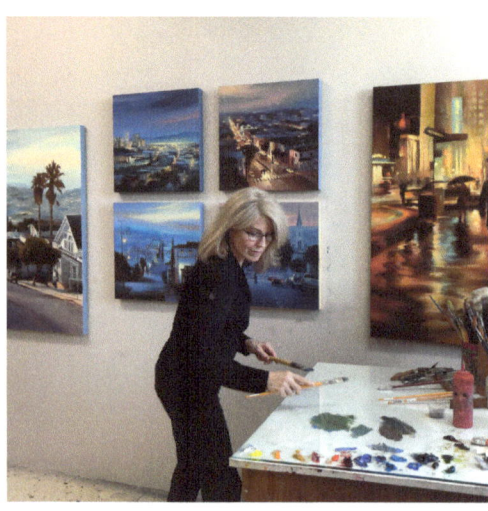

Seduced by the dramatic magnitude of San Francisco, I continue to fall under its spell and paint even more cityscapes. This 7 x 7 city is a visual feast, with its varied topography, diversity of microclimates, and ever-changing moods affected by sea fog, rainfall, sunshine, and marine air. Foggy nights are my favorite time when sensory details melt into the shadows to create formless abstractions.

My paintings are a visual diary of my life, representing places seen and emotions felt. I paint alone in my studio only accompanied by my favorite music—the mood of the music shows up in my paintings. If you were a fly on the wall, you might find me dancing between brushstrokes.

website: http://www.caroljessen.com/
email: carol@caroljessen.com

CAROL JESSEN was born and raised in Oakland, California. She received her BFA from San Francisco State University in journalism and biology. After graduating she donned her backpack and traveled around the world including Europe, Iran, Afghanistan, Pakistan, India and many countries of the Far East. She then attended Mendocino Art Center and the Academy of Art in San Francisco. Enticed by the far east, she moved to Kyoto, Japan for a year to learn the technique of Japanese woodblock printing and later went on to study under master printer, Toshi Yoshida. She was also tutored in design, composition and the psychology of perception by William S. Lansberg. She has lectured and performed woodblock demonstrations at Stanford University, the de Young Museum and the Asian Art Museum.

She worked as a "pre-computer" graphic designer and illustrator until saving up enough money to stop working and find a studio where she could devote herself to fine art. Hunters Point Shipyard, the once abandoned naval shipyard in San Francisco, is where Carol enjoys her studio by the bay. Her primary mediums are oil painting and various forms of printmaking and collage. Her work was featured at the New York Art Expo in 2004 by Editions Limited where her original oil paintings and pastels sold out. Her work is in the permanent collections of the Cleveland Museum and the New York Public Library collection

SELECT EXHIBITIONS

2016	*FourSquared VII*, Arc Gallery, San Francisco CA
2015	*FourSquared VI*, Arc Gallery, San Francisco CA
1995	Castle Fine Art, San Francisco, CA (solo)
1994	Stanford University, Palo Alto, CA (solo)
1992	The Verne Collection, Cleveland, OH
1990	Fort Mason Art Center Gallery, San Francisco, CA
1988	Fort Mason Art Center Gallery, San Francisco, CA

SELECTED GALLERIES & OTHER EXHIBITION VENUES

1988 -present	San Francisco Open Studios at Hunters Point Shipyard, 1988-present
1987-2010	Sausalito Arts Festival, Sausalito, CA (1987 to 2010) Juried (1994 Poster commission)
1990-1997	Mill Valley Arts Festival, Mill Valley, CA (1990 - 1997) Juried
	The Ren Brown Gallery, Bodega, CA
	Chemers Gallery, Anaheim, CA
	Studio Gallery, San Francisco, CA
	Joanne Chappel Gallery, San Francisco, CA
	Michael Thompson Gallery, San Francisco, CA

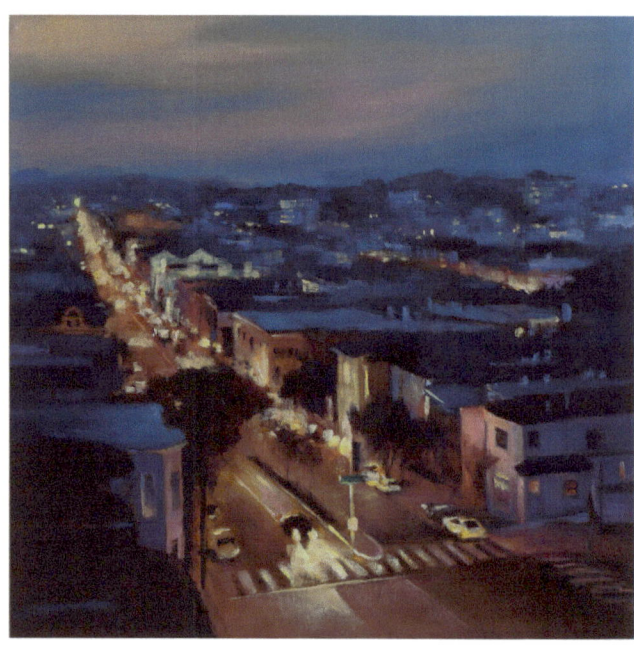

Divisadero
oil on wood panel
20" x 20"
$900

Frisco by the Bay
oil on wood panel
20" x 20"
$900

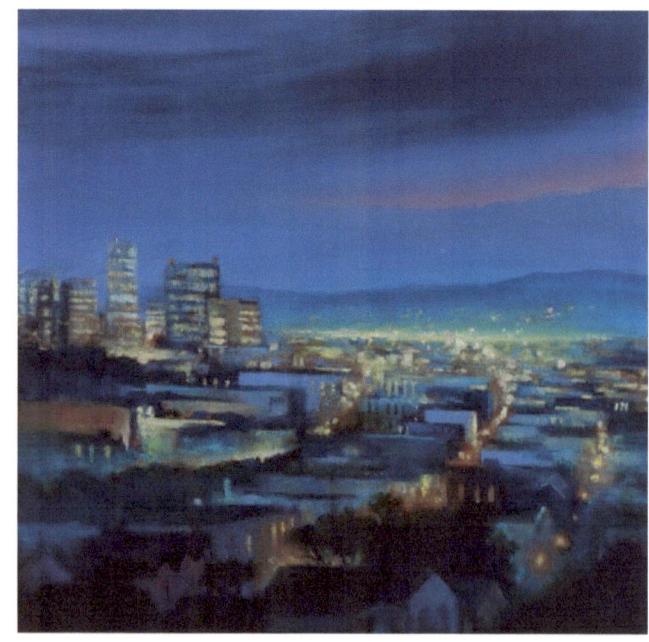

Carol Jessen

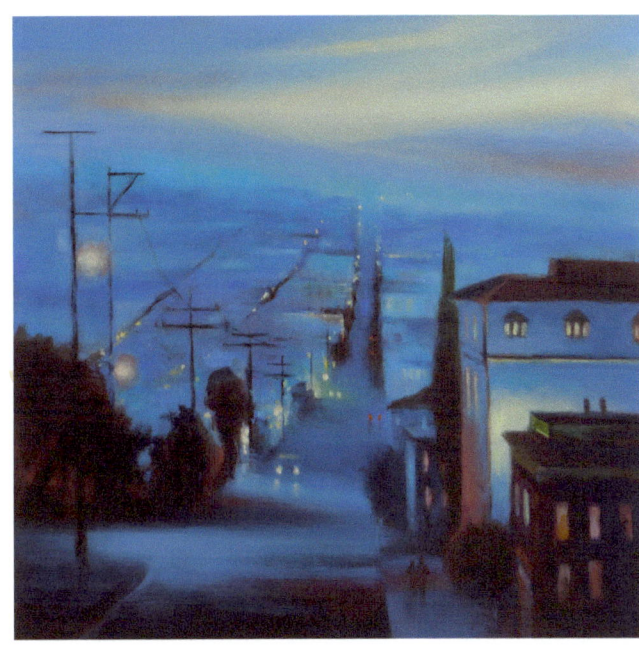

Fog Over San Francisco
oil on wood panel
20" x 20"
$900

Bayview
oil on wood panel
20" x 20"
$900

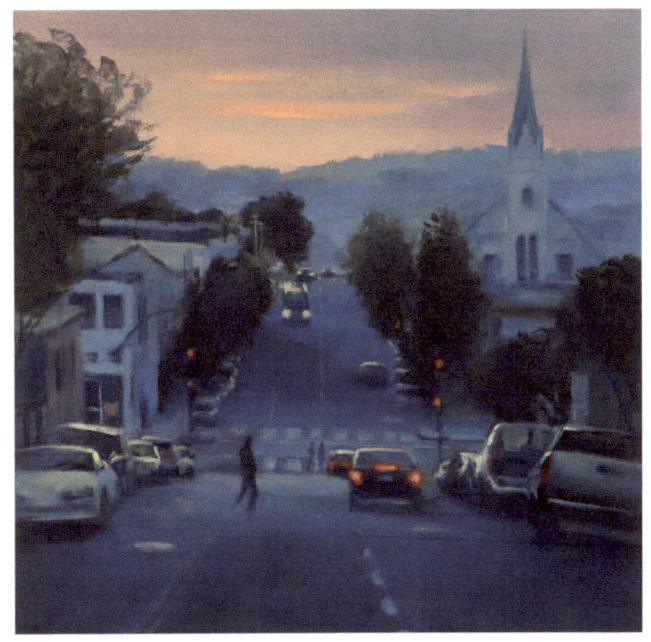

Carol Jessen

Margaret Keelan

Tiny Dancers

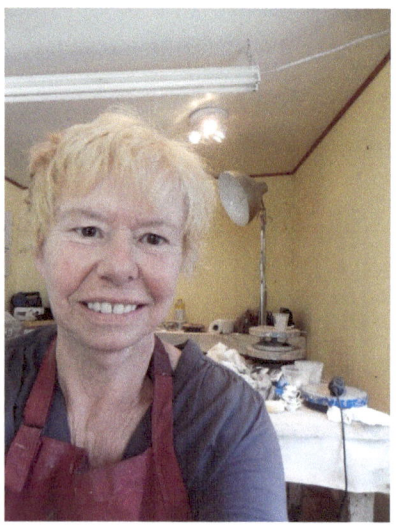

For the past few years, my sculptures have been repeatedly glazed, stained, and fired to give the surfaces the look of disintegrating paint over weathered wood. This softening and reduction of form so that its essential nature is revealed is a metaphor I use for a life being lived, an exploration of the process of growing up and growing older. I love the combination of innocence, trust and openness, combined with the knowingness and authenticity of an older age.

These small pieces are lighthearted and fun as they cavort across the wall—showing a childlike joyfulness and freshness, yet they also have the appearance of ancient little creatures that have been discovered and then dug up from deep in the earth.

website: http://www.margaretkeelan.com/
email: margaretkeelan@hotmail.com

MARGARET KEELAN is an internationally acclaimed, San Pablo-based sculptor. She has exhibited extensively since 1988; has received numerous awards and residencies; and is widely collected by museums, corporations and individuals.

EDUCATION

1976	M.F.A., Ceramic Sculpture, University of Utah, Salt Lake City, Utah
1970	Advanced B.A., Fine Arts, University of Saskatchewan, Saskatoon CAnada

RECENT EXHIBITIONS

2018	*The Spectrum of Women*, Gail Severn Gallery, Sun Valley, ID
	Deconstructing the Conversation, Morgan Glass Gallery, Pittsburgh, PA
2017	*Margaret Keelan, New Work*, Imprint Gallery, Cannon Beach OR
	Connection/Communion, Gail Severn Gallery, Sun Valley, ID
	Academy of Art University, School of Fine Art Sculpture Faculty Show, Atelier Gallery, San Francisco, CA
2016	*Strictly Figurative*, NCECA, Carter Art Center, Kansas City,.MO
	The Figure in Ceramic Art Series 2016, Intimate and Universal: The Figure Forward, Manhiem Gallery, Cottonwood, AZ
	FourSquared VIII, Arc Gallery, San Francisco, CA
	Narrative Ceramic Sculpture , Cannon Beach Gallery, Cannon Beach, OR
2015	*The September Show*, Abrams Claghorn Gallery, Albany, CA
	Figuratively Speaking, SMAart Gallery, San Francisco, CA
	Bodies and Beings, Abmeyer and Wood, Seattle, CA
	Fanciful Histories, (solo), Gail Severn Gallery, Sun Valley, ID
	Bark, John Natsoulas Gallery, Davis, CA
	Honoring the Past, Embracing the Future, American Museum of Ceramic Art, 10th Anniversary Show, Pomona, CA
2014	*Margaret Keelan* (solo), Roscoe Ceramic Gallery, Oakland, CA
	Some Pretty Interesting Characters: Works From the RAM Collection, Racine Art Museum, Racine, WI
2013	*The Essential and the Ephemeral* (solo), Gail Severn Gallery Sun Valley, ID
	Margaret Keelan, New Selections (solo), Duane Reed Gallery, St Louis, MI
2012	*Preview*, Gail Severn Gallery, Ketchum, Sun Valley, ID
	Red Dot Art Fair, Duane Reed Gallery, Miami, Florida
	SOFA Chicago, Duane Reed Gallery, Chicago, IL
	Ecumene: Global Interface in American Ceramics, Santa Fe, NM
	Figurative Works in Clay, Grover Thurston Gallery, Seattle, WA
	Push Play, NCECA Invitational, Bellevue Art Museum, Bellevue, WA

RECENT PUBLICATIONS

2014	*500 Figures in Clay, Volume 2"*, Lark Books
2012	*Ceramics and the Human Figure*, Edith Garcia, A & C Black Publishers Ltd.
2011	*Margaret Keelan • Profile*, Cheryl Coon New Ceramics, The European Ceramics Magazine, May/June
2009	*Confrontational Ceramics*, Judith Schwartz, , University of Pennsylvania Press, Philadelphia
2008	*Illuminations, Ones To Watch, Margaret Keelan*, Western Art and Architecture, Winter/Spring, Vol. 2, No. 1

TEACHING EXPERIENCE

1997 -	Associate Director of Sculpture, Academy of Art University, San Francisco, CA
1991	Advanced Ceramics and Figure Sculpture, San Francisco State University, San Francisco CA
1984-85	Figure Sculpture, Richmond Art Center Richmond, CA

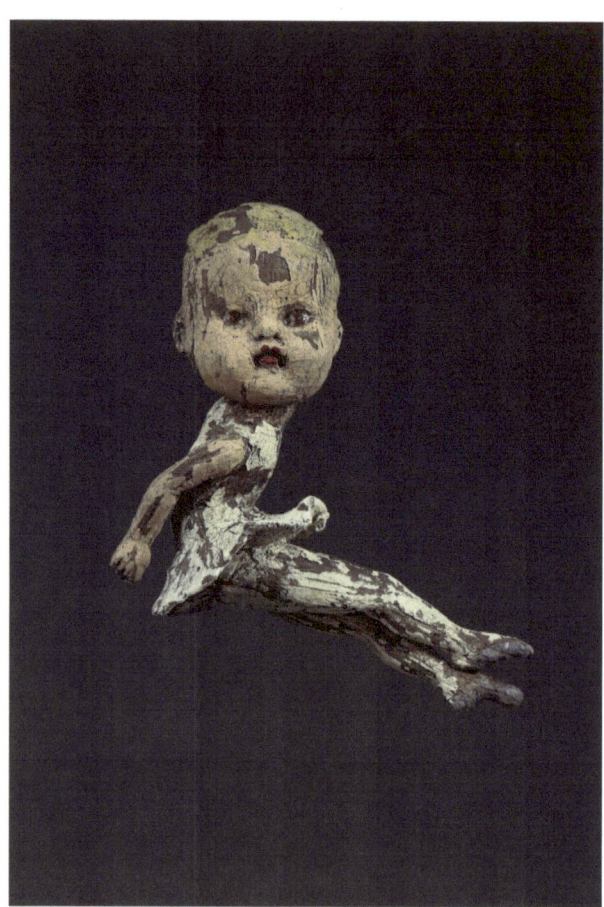

Tiny Dancer 1
ceramic
5" x 5"
$400

Tiny Dancer 2
ceramic
7" x 4"
$400

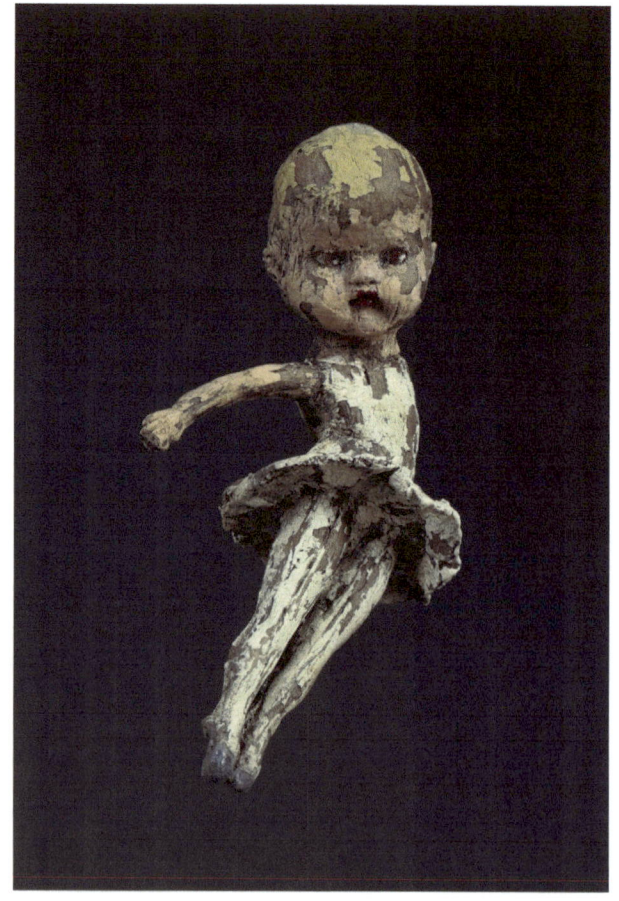

Margaret Keelan

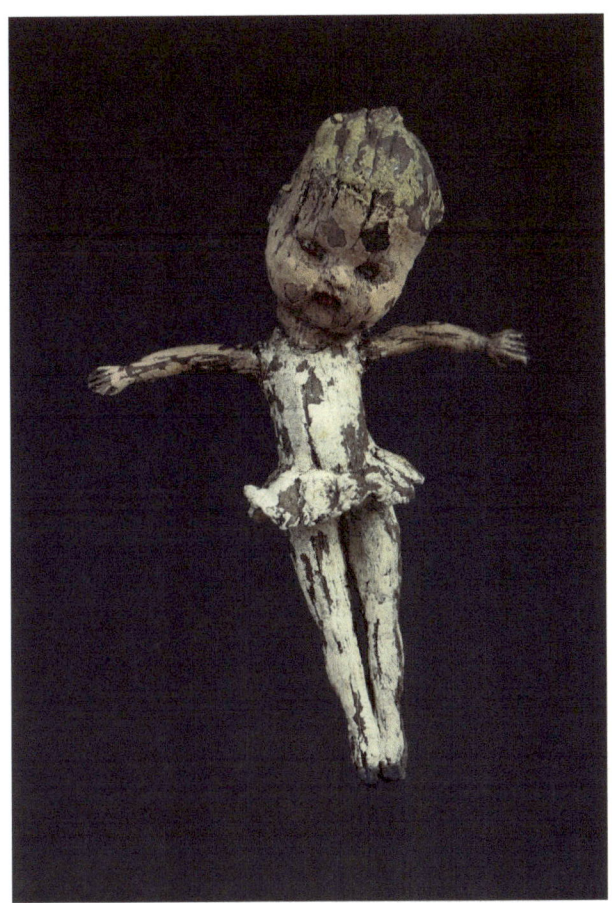

Tiny Dancer 3
ceramic
8" x 5"
$400

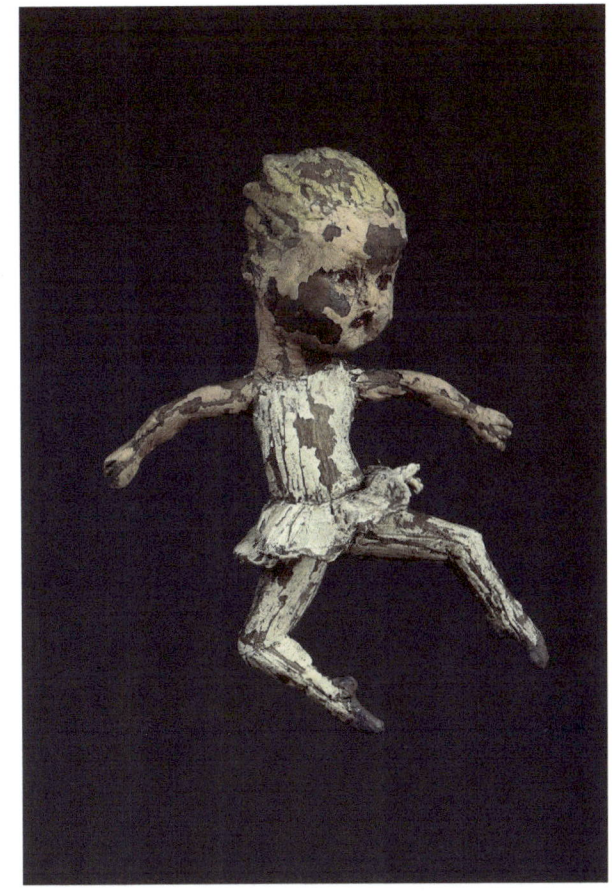

Tiny Dancer 4
ceramic
8" x 5"
$400

Margaret Keelan

Michael McConnell

Rancho San Antonio

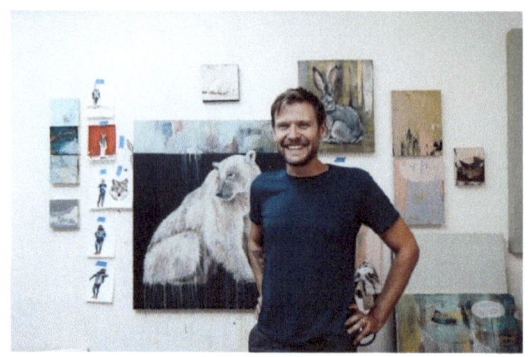

Observing my own anxieties and awkwardness, I create visual narratives that explore independence, responsibility and choice. I use animals to be the voice of innocence and vulnerability, emerging from abstracted environments.

website: http://michaelmcconnellart.com/
email: poopingrabbit@yahoo.com

photo credit: Jen Woo

EDUCATION

1999   BFA, Columbus College of Art and Design

RECENT SOLO EXHIBITIONS

2018	*California, I Love You,* Long Weekend, Oakland, CA
2016	*Introvert/Extrovert,* Blackbird, San Francisco, CA
	You Are Here, Marion and Rose's Workshop, Oakland, CA
2015	*Domesticity,* Julia Martin Gallery, Nashville, TN
2014	*Cozy,* Marion and Rose's Workshop, Oakland, CA
2013	*Infinitely Bound,* Interface Gallery, Oakland, Ca
2012	*Games Children Play,* Marion and Rose's Workshop, Oakland, CA
2011	*Tethered,* Braunstein/Quay, San Francisco, CA

RECENT GROUP EXHBITIONS

2018	*California Varietals,* Baana, San Francisco, CA
	Audio Visual, Nahcotta Gallery, Portsmouth NH
	Cultivated Nature, Mills Building, San Francisco, C
2017	*FourSquared,* Arc Gallery, San Francisco, CA
	ARC, Nacotta Gallery, Portsmouth, NH
	Sweet and Low, Bedford Gallery, Walnut Creek, CA
2016	*Enormous Tiny Art 19,* Nahcotta Gallery, Portsmouth, NH
2015	*September Show,* Abrams Claghorn, Albany, CA
	Strike Away Paxton Gate, San Francisco, CA
2014	*Contemporary/ Contemporary,* Guantlet Gallery, San Francisco, CA
	SquaredAlumni, Arc Gallery, San Francisco, CA
	CA 12x12, Gauntlet Gallery, San Francisco, CA
2013	*Bestiary,* Smart Clothes Gallery, New York, NY
	Peaceable Kingdom, Bedford Gallery, Walnut Creek, CA
2012	*BE:E,* La Porte Peinte, Noyers, France
	Captured: Specimens in Contemporary Art, Bedford Gallery, Walnut Creek, CA
	Myths of Progress, Kala Art Institute, Berkeley, CA
	Retrofit, Arc Gallery, San Francisco, CA
2011	*FourSquared,* Arc Gallery, San Francisco, CA
	CaliforNoyers, La Porte Peinte, Noyers, France

BIBLIOGRAPHY

25 Artists to Watch, Watercolor Magazine, Fall 2011
100 Artists of the West Coast II, Tina Skinner, Schiffer Publishing, 2009
New American Paintings 79: Juried by Ritz Gonzalez

ACADEMIC APPOINTMENTS & LECTURES

Residency at LPP, Noyers France
Eastern Oregon University, Visiting Lecture
2008 SECA Award nominee
Columbus State University, GA, Visiting Lecture and Demo
UC Berkley, Visiting Lecture in Painting

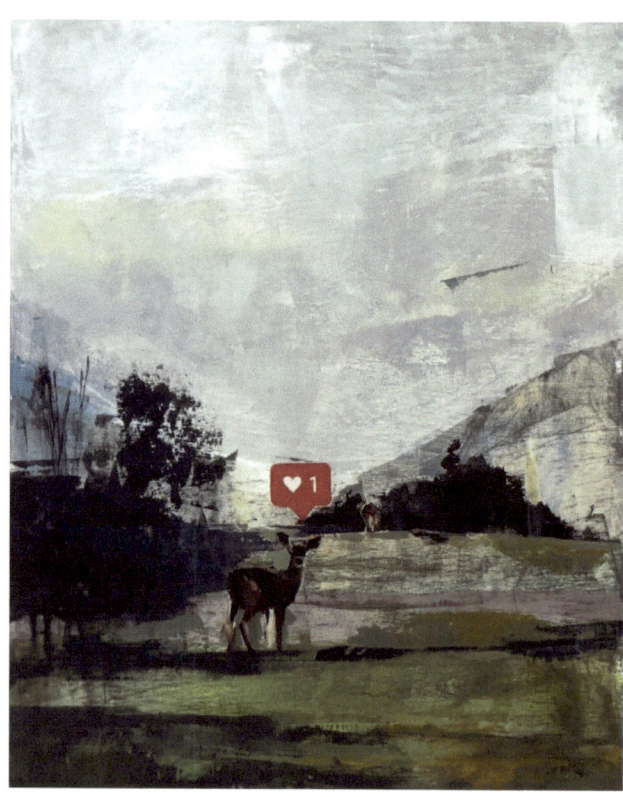

Double Tap
acrylic on wood panel
20" x 16"
$1125

Follow Me Back
acrylic on wood panel
20" x 16"
$1125

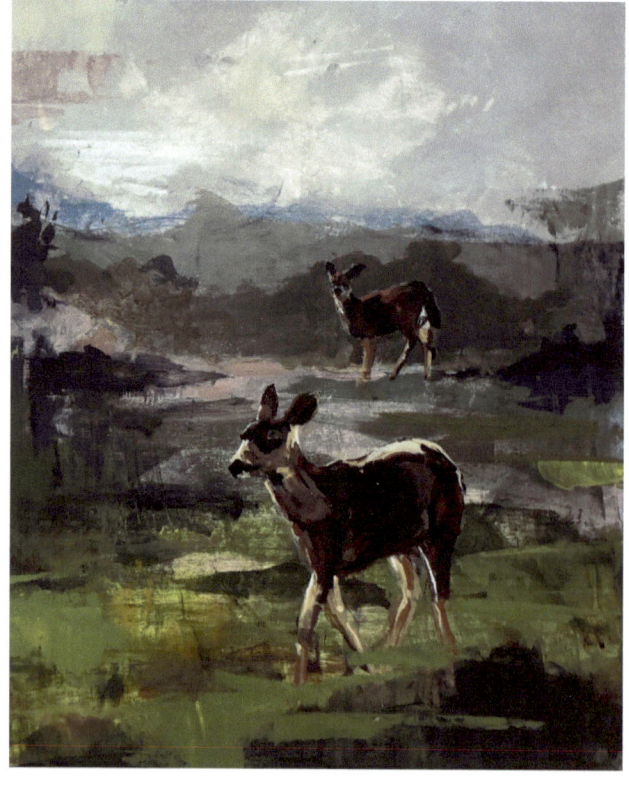

Michael McConnell

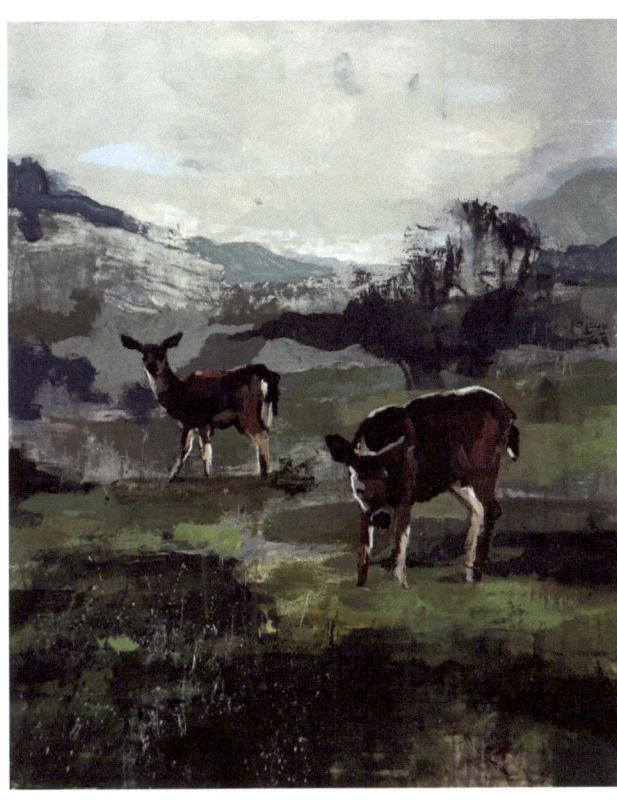

#MoraTrail
acrylic on wood panel
20" x 16"
$1125

Selfie
acrylic on wood panel
20" x 16"
$1125

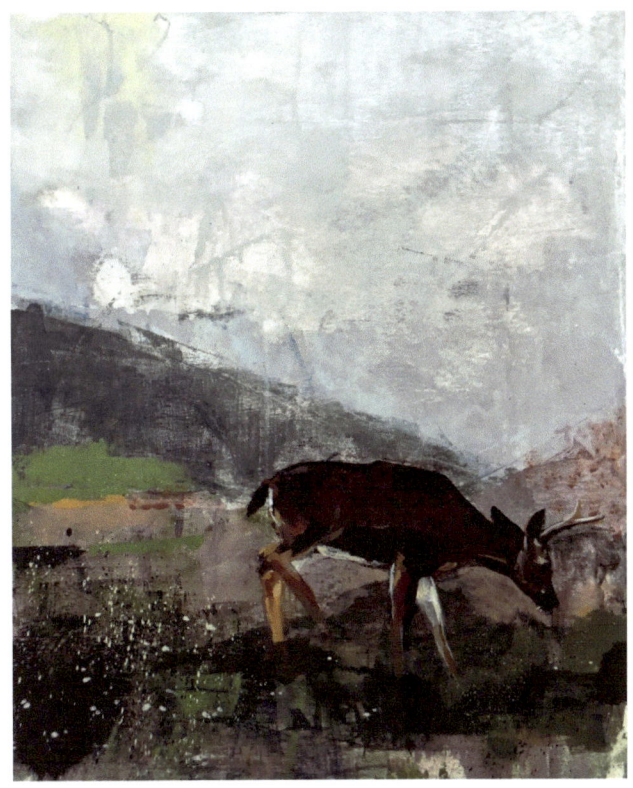

Michael McConnell

Sawyer Rose

Polarity

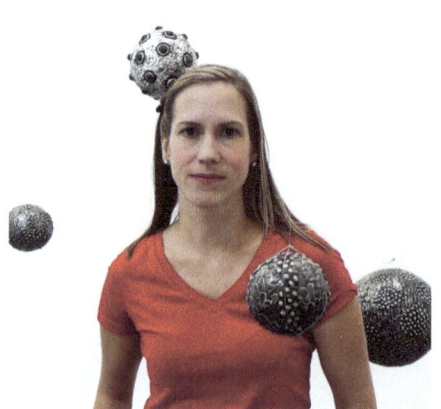

The spherical forms of my metalworks explore the ways living things adapt to changing environments. Clad in layers of silver solder and copper, their delicate bodies seem to grow the armor they need to flourish in the environment humans are leaving for them. Using the texture of the metal as my primary mark-making medium, the liquefied silver morphs into bark, or feathers, or scales.

website: http:// www.sawyerrose.com
email: sawyer@sawyerrose.com

SAWYER ROSE is a sculpture, installation, and social practice artist. Born and raised in North Carolina and a graduate of Williams College in Massachusetts, she currently lives and works in the San Francisco Bay Area. Throughout her career, Sawyer has used her artwork to shine a spotlight on contemporary social and ecological issues. She is also the President of the Northern California Women's Caucus for Art.

RECENT SOLO & TWO-PERSON EXHIBITIONS

2017	*Force of Nature*, from The Carrying Stones Project, Classic Cars West Gallery, Oakland, CA. (solo)
2016	*Ties That Bind*, from the Carrying Stones Project, Fort Mason Center for Arts & Culture, San Francisco, CA (solo)
	Surface & Strata, GearBox Gallery, Oakland, CA
2015	*Seeds of the Monoliths*, Room Art Gallery, Mill Valley, CA
	Flux, Classic Cars West Gallery with Chandra Cerrito Contemporary, Oakland, CA (solo)
2012-14	*Dusk to Dawn*, Inclusions Gallery, San Francisco, CA (solo)
	Marin Headlands Visitors Center, Sausalito, CA (solo)
	NATIVE: California Plants in Metal, Glass & Light, Inclusions Gallery, San Francisco, CA (solo)

RECENT GROUP EXIBITIONS

2018	Art Market San Francisco, 2 main floor on-site installations
	SCOPE art fair, New York, NY
	Art on Paper art fair, New York, NY
	CK Contemporary, San Francisco, CA
	Make Your Mark, Marin Museum of Contemporary Art, Novato, CA
2017	*Currently 80*, with Sculptors Guild, Westbeth Gallery, New York, NY
	Selections 2017, with ArtSpan SF, Heron Arts, San Francisco, CA
	Wood, Metal & Memory, 3-artist exhibition, Inclusions Gallery, San Francisco, CA
	American Twist, Antenna Gallery, New Orleans, LA
2016	Room Art Gallery, Mill Valley, CA
	Chandra Cerrito Contemporary, Oakland, CA
	Art Market San Francisco, San Francisco, CA
	The Alchemist, Root Division, San Francisco, CA
	Abstract Sanctuary, Verum Ultimum Gallery, Portland, OR
2015	Chandra Cerrito Contemporary, Oakland, CA
	14th National Prize Show, Kathryn Schultz Gallery, Cambridge Art Assn., Cambridge, MA
	Hilton Head Biennial, Walter Greer Gallery, Hilton Head, SC

SELECTED GRANTS & RESIDENCIES

2018	The Ragdale Foundation, Lake Forest, IL
2017	Massachusetts Museum of Contemporary Art, North Adams, MA
	The Awesome Foundation Grant
2016	The Tyrone Guthrie Centre at Annaghmakerrig, Newbliss, Co. Monaghan, Ireland
	Fort Mason Center for Arts & Culture, San Francisco, CA
	Penland School of Crafts, Penland, NC
	Vermont Studio Center, Johnson, Vermont
2014	Center for Cultural Innovation, Creative Capacity Fund
	Vermont Studio Center residency and grant
2013	Vermont Studio Center residency and grant

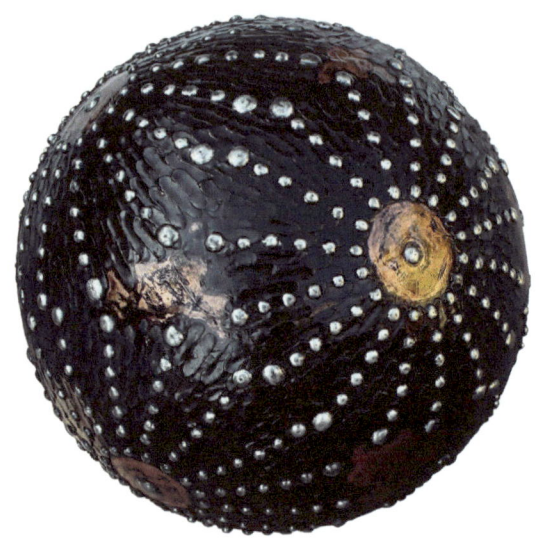

Dissent
silver solder and copper over rigid foam
10" diameter
$2800

Majority
silver solder and copper over rigid foam
8" diameter
$1800

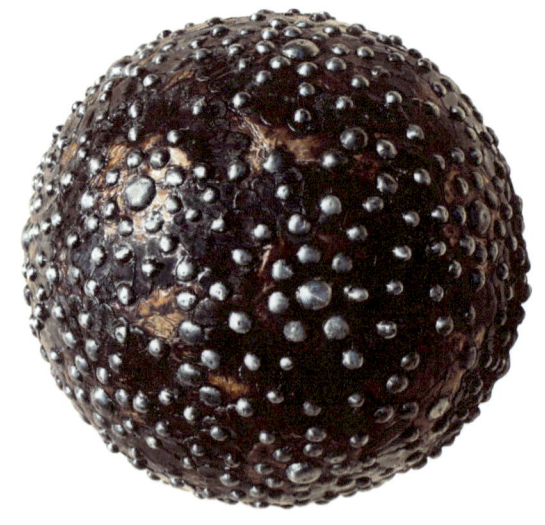

Sawyer Rose

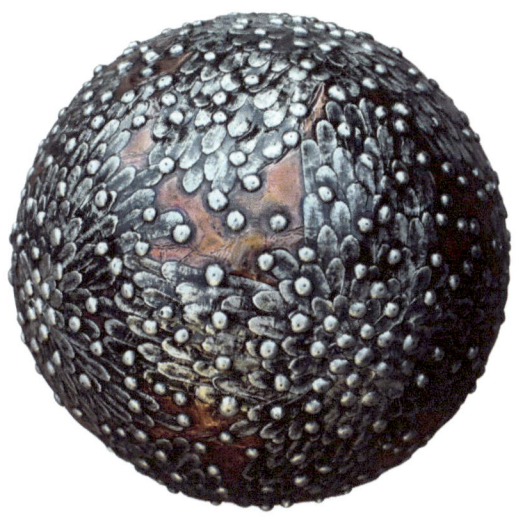

Sol
silver solder and copper over rigid foam
6" diameter
$980

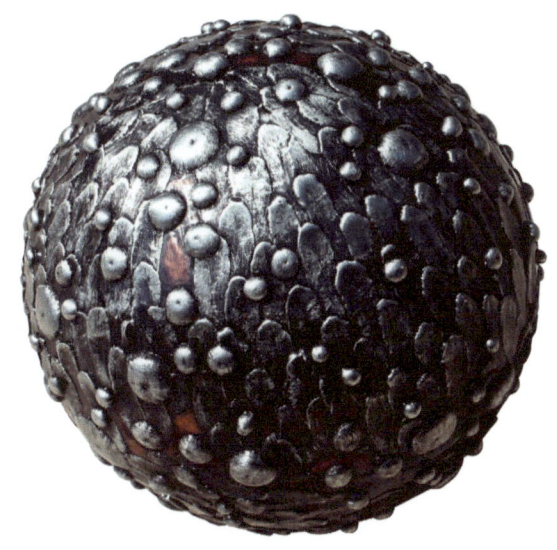

Luna
silver solder and copper over rigid foam
4.5" diameter
$580

Sawyer Rose

Charles Stinson

Essential Devices

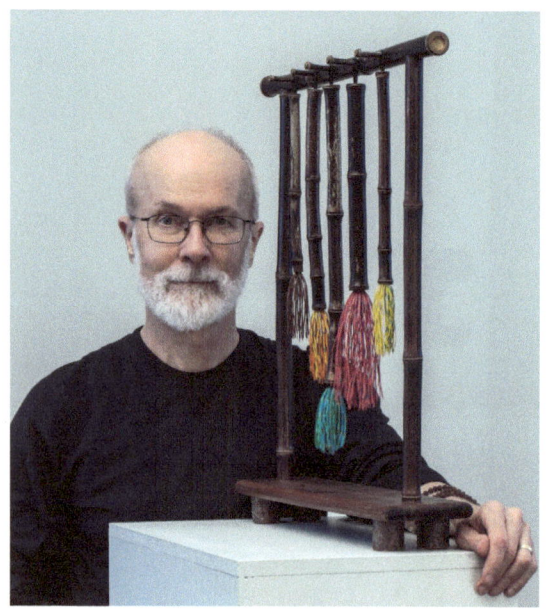

I have always worked in a broad range of media and explored a variety of techniques, so studio visitors often assume my works are by multiple artists.

What connects and is constant across the works is their multi-layered depth — of thought, questioning, and story — which combine to create a resonance of meaning, inviting gaze and thought to linger.

This series continues explorations of accelerating changes in our world — including what objects, skills, meanings or values are preserved, repurposed, misunderstood, distorted, or simply cast aside and forgotten.

website: http://charlesstinson.com/
email: charlesstinson@me.com

CHARLES H. STINSON's multi-faceted creations take shape in his space at 1890 Bryant Street Studios in San Francisco, California. Born and raised in Texas, he moved to San Francisco in 1978. He is current president of Pacific Rim Sculptors (PRS), a chapter of the International Sculpture Center.

EDUCATION

Studies at the Houston Museum of Art School of Art
Japanese calligraphy with Sensei Shioh Kato, San Francisco, CA
Traditional & photogravure etching techniques at Crown Point Press, San Francisco, CA
Largely self-directed learning

SELECTED EXHIBITIONS

2018	*Room for Thought*, SPACE 151, San Francisco, CA (juror: Jack Fisher)
	International Sculpture Center, Zona Maco, Mexico City, Mexico (juried digital exhibition)
	Forms & Sequences, Siskiyou Arts Museum, Dunsmuir, CA (juror: Phil Linhares)
2017	International Sculpture Center, Miami Art Fair, Miami, FL (juried digital exhibition)
	International Sculpture Center, EXPO Chicago, IL (juried digital exhibition)
	FourSquared VIII, Arc Gallery, San Francisco, CA
2016	*Pacific Rim Sculptors: International Sculpture Day,* Art Object Gallery, San Jose, CA
2015	*Soul Season: Works by Charles H. Stinson*, a.Muse Gallery, San Francisco, CA
	California Sculpture SLAM, CCS & San Luis Obispo Museum of Art, San Luis Obispo, CA
	The Left Coast, Western Regional show sponsored by Marin Society of Artists, Marin, CA
2013	*Discarted – Art from Trash*, Ojai Art Festival Juried Exhibition. Ojai, CA
	Wisdom 2.0: Mindfulness, Wisdom and Compassion in the Technology Age; San Francisco, CA; Will Chase, Curator.
	Beyond Gaga, Pacific Rim Sculptors, Works Gallery, San Jose, CA
2008	*75th Annual Awards Exhibition*, National Sculpture Society, New York, NY
	75th Annual Awards Exhibition, Brookgreen Gardens, Pawleys Island, SC
2004	*Off the Rim*, Grounds for Sculpture, Hamilton, NJ; Brooke Barrie, Curator
1985	*Senkei International Calligraphy Competition*, Tokyo, Japan. Certificate of Special Merit

SELECTED PUBLICATIONS

2017	*Devices of Dubious Utility from the Museum of Post-Truth Artifacts*, Charles H. Stinson, Starchand Press, San Francisco, CA
2016	*A Gristly Tail*, Charles H. Stinson, Starchand Press, San Francisco, CA
2012	*Hot Poems for Warm Friends,* George Paris. C. H. Stinson, editor, Starchand Press, San Francisco, CA
2004	*In Three Dimensions: Twelve sculptors speak out about self-expression in their chosen media*, Norman Kolpas, Southwest Art

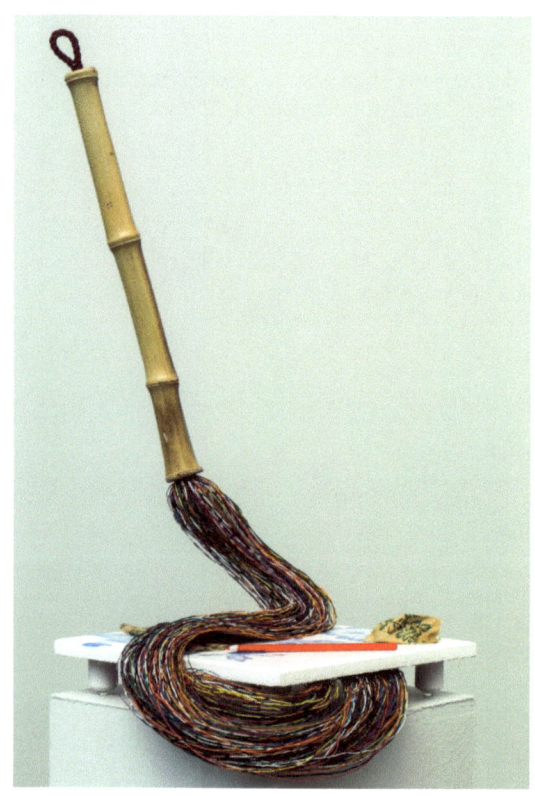

Fake Brush for Describing the Commodity of Truth
mixed media, bamboo, wire, wood, acrylic, paper
27" x 16"x 16"
$1450

Autonomous Device for Managing Road Rage
mixed media, bamboo, found objects, travertine
17.5" x 29"x 5"
$1350

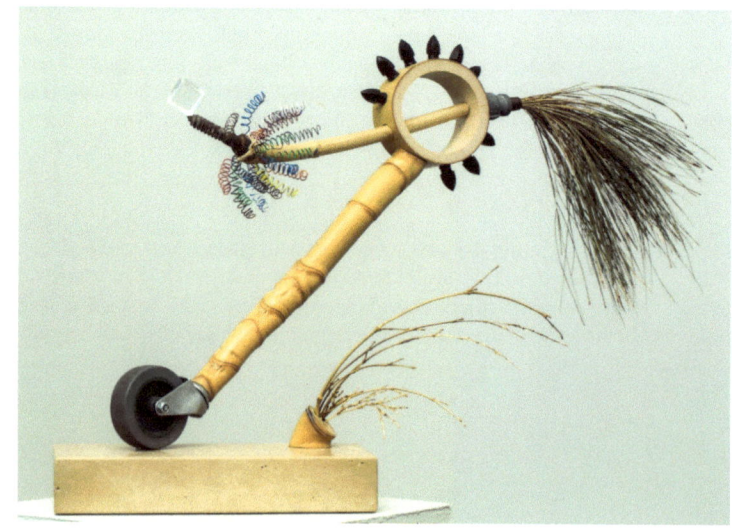

Charles Stinson

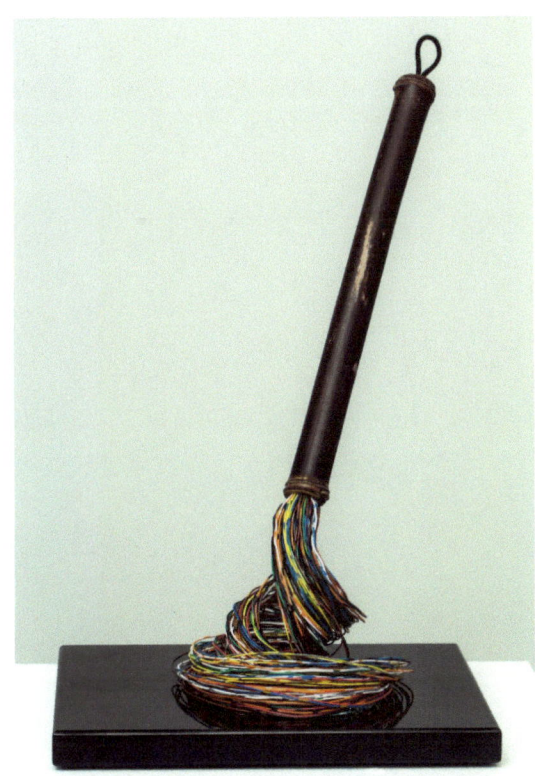

PNG Brush
mixed media, bamboo, wire
14" x 8" x 11"
$725

Brushes for Painting Digital Dreams
mixed media, bamboo, wire
22" x 18.75" x 4.25"
$1250

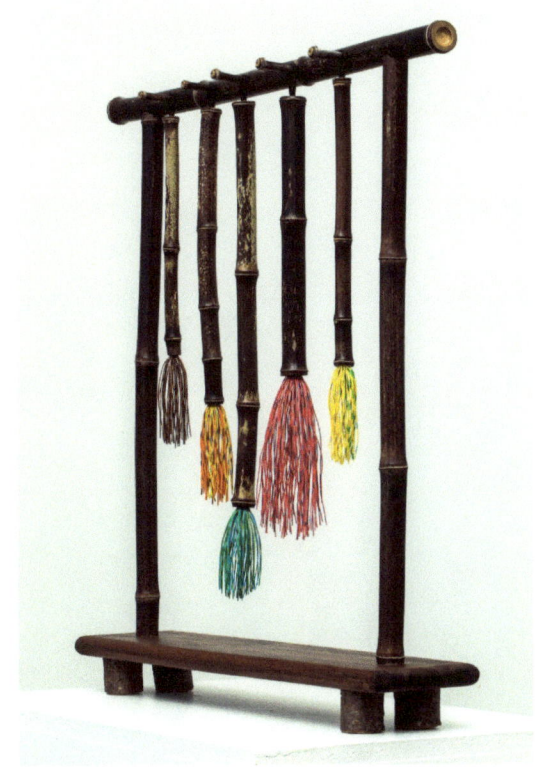

Charles Stinson

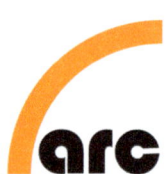

gallery
project gallery
studios
fine art consulting

1246 Folsom St.
San Francisco, CA

http://arc-sf.com
http://arcfinearts-sf.com
arcgallerysf@gmail.com
415-298-7969